this Isn't 40

~~this isn't~~ to

A PLAY BY

SCOTT CAAN

A Genuine Rare Bird Book • Los Angeles, Calif.

THIS IS A GENUINE RARE BIRD BOOK

Rare Bird Books
453 South Spring Street, Suite 302
Los Angeles, CA 90013
rarebirdlit.com

FIRST HARDCOVER EDITION

Set in Dante
Printed in the United States.

10 9 8 7 6 5 4 3 2 1

Publisher's Cataloging-in-Publication Data
available on request

CAST OF CHARACTERS

ROSE, early thirties
JIMMY, late thirties–early forties
DONNIE, late thirties–early forties
BINKI, early twenties
MONICA, early twenties

SETTINGS

Jimmy's Living Room

PRODUCTION NOTES

The entire play takes place at night, except the very last scene, and spans over a seven-year period. Lights, wardrobe, and wigs inform change in time. There should not be an intermission. Slick and seamless set changes are okay during blackouts between scenes. For example, Jimmy might remove art from the walls and replace them with paintings that his daughter may have painted. There should not be any visible set hands on stage during the performance. Anything that happens should be live on stage, and handled by the cast as the characters in the play.

ACKNOWLEDGMENTS

Bob, Kathleen, Bre, Val, Mia, Marley, and Mathew.

ACT ONE

SCENE 1

It's night time. Open floor plan. Living room flows into the kitchen and dining area. Small bar, up right. Nice Place.

Artists home. Books on shelves, no television, paintings on the walls. Comfortable but modern and nothing out of place. Could be a living room, or the show room of a furniture store. But done right. Very sexy and tasteful.

JIMMY enters with ROSE. She wears a BBQ-soiled shirt.

JIMMY

Don't move. I'll be right back.

ROSE

Okay.

Jimmy heads for a door, up left, but then stops and turns back.

JIMMY

Feel free to move.

ROSE

What?

JIMMY

You don't have to stay frozen in time.

ROSE

Got it. Thanks.

He exits.

Rose takes off the BBQ-soiled shirt revealing skin and bra. She places the shirt on a chair and moves around the room taking in the details.

Jimmy steps back out holding a vintage Harley-Davidson T-shirt. Rose doesn't bother covering herself. Jimmy, frozen by the site moves forward nonetheless.

JIMMY

Wow.

ROSE

Sorry.

JIMMY

No. Please. Here. Try this.

She takes a look at the shirt he brought out, holds it up, and smiles.

ROSE

Thanks.

Rose puts the shirt on while Jimmy grabs the dirty shirt, folds it, and sets it back down.

JIMMY

I had a really good time tonight.

ROSE

I did, too.

JIMMY

Sorry about the little accident.

                           ROSE

You made her nervous.

                          JIMMY

The waitress?

                           ROSE

Yes. The waitress.

                          JIMMY

I didn't make her nervous.

He moves for a Record Player that rests on the credenza.

                           ROSE

She spilled an entire plate of BBQ wings on my head.

                          JIMMY

She handles food for a living. Mistakes happen.

He spins a record, then moves back over to her.

                           ROSE

Not like that they don't. Trust me. I know. You make women
nervous.

                          JIMMY

What can I say?

                           ROSE

You're charming.

Jimmy dims the lights a bit.

                          JIMMY

No. You're charming. The way you handled it. You could
have made her feel horrible about the whole thing and you
didn't. Says a lot.

ROSE

My mother was a waitress. Bunch of kids. Lotta work.
I understand.

JIMMY

I see.

ROSE

You?

JIMMY

Methadone addict.

ROSE

Excuse me?

JIMMY

My mother. Just kidding. Sort of.

Jimmy lights a few candles.

ROSE

I meant do you have any siblings?

JIMMY

Ah. No. Just me. Both parents are gone now too, so really
just me.

Jimmy moves for the bar.

ROSE

My parents have been married thirty-five years.

JIMMY

Wow.

ROSE

I'm sorry, I don't know why I just said that.

JIMMY

I imagine probably because it's true… Drink?

ROSE

You trying to get me drunk?

JIMMY

One hundred percent.

Rose keeps her eyes on Jimmy as he mixes the drinks.

ROSE

You know, you seem like you're doing a thing.

JIMMY

A thing?

ROSE

Yes.

JIMMY

What kind of a thing?

ROSE

Like a well-rehearsed thing.

JIMMY

I'm certainly not doing a thing.

ROSE

Can you stop it?

He brings the drink over to her.

JIMMY

Maybe…I'm doing a thing.

ROSE

Thank you for saying that.

JIMMY

Thank you for pointing it out. I'll stop.

He hands her the drink.

ROSE

It's not necessary.

JIMMY

I agree. I just said I'll stop.

He moves to the record player and stops it.

ROSE

Great. Now that we've pushed past that with a certain amount of ease, you mind if I ask you some questions?

JIMMY

Not at all. I like questions.

ROSE

Great. I hope I like your answers.

JIMMY

Yeah. Me, too.

She takes a sip of her drink.

ROSE

You sleep around?

JIMMY

Jesus.

ROSE

You like kids?

JIMMY

Jesus.

ROSE

They're just questions. I'm not much for wasting time. I know what I like. Do these questions make you uncomfortable?

JIMMY

One.

ROSE

One what?

JIMMY

One kid. I'd like. Me. Sleep around's too vague, so I can't answer that.

ROSE

That's good.

JIMMY

I'm not a virgin.

ROSE

That's very good.

JIMMY

And the kid question didn't make me uncomfortable, although it should have. Sort of turned me on somehow.

ROSE

That's hot.

                            JIMMY

Right?

                             ROSE

And kind of gross if you think about it.

                            JIMMY

You're different. You know that?

                             ROSE

Like a rare bird?

                            JIMMY

Something like that.

                             ROSE

Different than you, you mean?

                            JIMMY

That too, probably.

She leans in. Studies him a bit.

                            JIMMY

What?

                             ROSE

Well, you know the way I see it…you throw ten people in a
room and give them a problem that needs to be solved, let's
say they're all violent, chances are they're gonna come up
with something along the lines of, what the fuck, let's just
kill everyone, right?

                            JIMMY

Sure.

ROSE

That's no good.

JIMMY

No. Death sucks.

ROSE

But you throw five pacifists in that same room with five of the crazies, chances are now, you might just come up with a more constructive and effective way to deal with the situation, don't you think?

JIMMY

I think so, yeah.

She studies him some more.

ROSE

Do you really, or are you just agreeing with me?

JIMMY

Can I tell you something?

ROSE

Sure, I like something.

JIMMY

You're kinda doing a thing.

ROSE

Oh God, really?

JIMMY

Little bit. But it's not necessary. You can stop it.

ROSE

You sure?

JIMMY

I'm ninety-nine point nine percent absolutely positive.

ROSE

I like you, too.

JIMMY

What?

ROSE

This shirt.

JIMMY

What about it?

ROSE

I know we just met, but you wouldn't give this shirt to a girl you weren't hoping to see again.

JIMMY

I just grabbed the first one off the top.

ROSE

No, you didn't. This one's special. "Says a lot."

JIMMY

Looks nice on you. Fits. Ya know?

ROSE

I like you, and I like your answers.

Jimmy leans in.

JIMMY

So what do you think? Can we sleep around a little bit?

ROSE

I imagine your sheets are amazing.

                         JIMMY
The best.

Rose leans in.

                         ROSE
You looking for something different, Jimmy?

                         JIMMY
I think I am. Yes.

                         ROSE
Well, I think I like that. But second base only, okay?

Jimmy moves in again. Even closer. Almost touching.

                         JIMMY
You know Rose, with the internet now, kids these days and
all that, I'm pretty sure second base could get you pregnant.

A kiss. Soft. Long. Nice.

LIGHTS OUT.

SCENE 2

DONNIE finishes making himself a drink, tosses it back, then begins to pace. Jimmy enters, hurried. He looks down at his watch.

JIMMY

Alright, what's up?

DONNIE

For the record, I don't even know this girl you're going out with and I hate her already.

JIMMY

I told you I had a few minutes when you got here. Now tell me what's up?

DONNIE

I'm sorry, but is that a real question?

JIMMY

Donnie.

DONNIE

No. It's just twice now you've asked it. Three if you count the pleasantries when I first arrived.

JIMMY

I want to help you Donnie.

DONNIE

Then stop looking at your watch and stop asking me questions you already know the answers to. What's up? I'm driving around looking for a tree to wrap my car around. That's what's up. Meanwhile, you gotta date that's apparently more important than my survival.

JIMMY

That's not true. Back to back in the alley. Come on.

DONNIE

Goddamn right back to back in the alley? But that's not the issue here is it, Jimmy? No. The issue here, is that like an asshole, against my sane and logical judgment, I extended said credit to that crooked gypsy and married her. Look at me now. Taking it right where I stand.

JIMMY

We've been over this.

DONNIE

Yeah, well obviously decision making hasn't been my strong suit when it comes to Lily, Jimmy. I might as well have been walking around with a sign denouncing the institution when I met her, like a goddamn activist, but here was this beautiful angel. This sweet, foreign, but fairly decent English-speaking young person, who for some reason or another smelled like pancakes all the time. That's right.

Lily. She smells like fresh dough and browned butter. What the fuck is that? I should have known something was suspect. Never trust anything that smells like breakfast. Noted. Got it. I'll make a sign. Get a tattoo. Whatever.

The point is, I was blinded by smells and body parts and like a pathetic dope I laid it all out on the line and said, hey you, you're with me. You, your ugly mother and that half retarded brother, another pair of things I should have payed more attention to, and further flagged as red, but I didn't because once again I'm an asshole. Instead, I said welcome. Everything I got, it's yours, you are with me in full, and I got you no matter what.

JIMMY

Yes.

DONNIE

Yes?

JIMMY

Yes, you did those things.

Jimmy checks his watch again.

DONNIE

You look at that watch one more time, I'm gonna eat it.

JIMMY

I'm right here, aren't I?

DONNIE

You really like this girl, don't you?

JIMMY

Not at all relevant, but yes I do. She's a nice girl. We have a nice time.

DONNIE

I'm sure that's how it seems.

JIMMY

Please, don't do that. You know how many second dates I've been on in my life?

DONNIE

What's her name?

JIMMY

Doesn't matter what her name is.

                    DONNIE

What does that mean?

                    JIMMY

It means nothing.

                    DONNIE

Tell me her name.

                    JIMMY

I don't want to.

Donnie gets in Jimmy's face.

                    JIMMY

Okay, her name is Rose.

                    DONNIE

Oh my God.

                    JIMMY

There's nothing there.

                    DONNIE

Her name is Rose?

                    JIMMY

I just told you there's nothing there.

                    DONNIE

Rose? My soon-to-be ex-wife's name is Lily, you're falling for
a Rose, and nothing is there, are you out of your mind?

                    JIMMY

This is not about me.

DONNIE

You're right. It's about evil presenting itself behind the disguise of pretty girls with sweet floral nomenclature?

You wanna live in the dark, go ahead, but you have been warned, my friend.

JIMMY

That's it. I'm leaving.

Jimmy grabs his jacket.

DONNIE

I'm drowning here, Jimmy. I'm literally up to here in dirty water and I can't see any light. I can't even breathe. The airs something else in here. You got the heat on?

Jimmy puts down the jacket.

JIMMY

What do you want me to do?

DONNIE

Just tell me what to do and I'll do it.

JIMMY

You know I can't do that?

DONNIE

Why not?

JIMMY

Because two weeks ago you were ready to throw Lily off a cliff. Last week you were gonna work it out. Today she's the devil. I can't push you toward a decision that one day you might regret, and somehow I'm responsible. I won't do that. It's your life.

DONNIE

She fucked the janitor, Jimmy.

JIMMY

I know that.

DONNIE

Another man, a custodian might I add, put his penis inside of my wife's pretty place, I'm considering being okay with it, and my best friend doesn't even have an opinion? This is clearly the end. Maybe I should just kill myself.

JIMMY

No, you shouldn't, but that's exactly what you're doing going back and forth with this thing. It's been months now. I know it's hard, and I'm sorry, and it sucks, but you gotta figure it out. One way or the other. That's my opinion. Pick and stick. That's it.

DONNIE

Did you just say pick and stick to me?

JIMMY

You have a decision to make.

DONNIE

Clearly a decision I'm having trouble making.

JIMMY

I understand that, but you still have to make it.

DONNIE

Well, what the hell do you think I'm doing here?

JIMMY

I don't know.

DONNIE

Help me, Jimmy.

JIMMY

Okay, I will. You remember Tony Testone?

DONNIE

What kinda question is that? I almost ran him over that night. On purpose. Hard to forget the guy. You don't still talk to him, do you?

JIMMY

I'm just trying to make a point here, okay.

DONNIE

Yeah? Show me something with a point so I can stick it in Lily's mother's ear. Fucking peasant. You know what I did to keep that little troll woman in this country?

JIMMY

I do. Yes I do.

DONNIE

They would have sent her back in a boat. Under the fuckin' thing, they would have sent her.

JIMMY

Tony Testone.

DONNIE

Asshole.

JIMMY

Whatever. He goes to Las Vegas. Ends up having sex with some Ukrainian Woman he met at a strip club—

DONNIE

Stripper?

JIMMY

No, she's a vacuum salesman… Yes, she's a stripper. Takes him in the back for a dance, one thing leads to another, these things happen, it's Vegas—

DONNIE

You don't gotta tell me. We could be there by midnight.

JIMMY

I have a date in seven minutes. I'm not going to Las Vegas.

DONNIE

You should cancel.

JIMMY

Listen to me.

DONNIE

Forever. Cancel 'em all.

JIMMY

Tony comes home to his wife. He feels guilty. He feels dirty. He's not happy with his behavior. So what does he do? He sits his wife down and tells her exactly what happened.

DONNIE

Told you that guy was an asshole.

JIMMY

Fine. Not up for debate. Giant asshole. But here's what happens. Here's where it gets interesting. What does Tony's wife do? She says okay.

DONNIE

Okay?

JIMMY

That's right. Okay? Not like it's okay that he did it, or not like, okay, let me think for a few seconds, pause, then tell you to get fucked, no. Okay. Period.

DONNIE

I don't get it.

JIMMY

Neither did Tony. At first. But what he slowly, over the next few months very clearly started to get, was what this woman, in that very short split second upon hearing the bad news, had already planned for our friend Tony.

DONNIE

Your friend, but go ahead, I'm listening.

JIMMY

Torture. Slow and very brutal torture. She had a card in her pocket that she would pull out at least once a day.

Pass the salt. Why, you wanna stick your dick in that too? Didn't matter. Tortured this man every chance she got, and still to this day continues. That's life over there now, and you ask me, that ain't no way to live. You think you got it in you to forgive and forget? Fine. If not? Call the fucking lawyer immediately. But it's gotta be one or the other. You see unfortunately, for everyone involved, Tony's wife couldn't make that decision. No. She landed somewhere else. The middle. The dirty ass middle. That horrid gray area, that when dealing with matters of the heart, turns the sane man into a fucking nut job. And it seems to me, that you my friend, have just recently decided to purchase property right next to the mayor's office.

DONNIE

So what, now I'm Tony Testone?

JIMMY

No. You're his wife in this particular setup. But who cares? That's not even the point. It don't matter who did what? You think she's any happier than he is today?

DONNIE

I hate 'em both.

JIMMY

Exactly. They're both miserable. Why?

DONNIE

Mayor's office?

JIMMY

That's right.

DONNIE

Your metaphors are like math code.

JIMMY

What can I say?

DONNIE

Aside from the fact that you've been sport fucking like an Olympian since puberty, and couldn't possibly understand the complexities of a real relationship, not much.

JIMMY

Fair enough. But you got two ways to live and learn in this life. You either do what you see or you do the exact opposite. I watched my folks go back and forth between love and hate for the better part of my early years until he finally decided to put a bullet in his head while she checked out on methadone lollypops.

DONNIE

You're literally a miracle.

JIMMY

You gotta pay attention.

DONNIE

Either that or hide the guns and lollypops.

JIMMY

Pick a side and stick with it. Period. Not for Lily's sake. For yours. You stay on the fence too long, that shit's gonna slice you right in half. That much I know for sure.

Jimmy checks his watch one last time.

JIMMY

I really gotta go.

He throws on his Jacket, and then checks himself out in the mirror.

DONNIE

I'm warning you, Jimmy. It all starts with a date.

Jimmy turns back to face Donnie.

DONNIE

Then you die… All the shit in the middle's a blur.

JIMMY

I really think there might be something here with this girl. It's obviously still very fresh but I'm slowly approaching forty, and I gotta be honest…it's time to try something different. For me. I got no choice.

DONNIE

Sure you do. Back to back in the alley?

JIMMY

Always.

DONNIE

Then don't leave me alone.

JIMMY

You're gonna be fine. I'm gonna be fine. This is life and we figure it out.

LIGHTS OUT

SCENE 3

ONE YEAR LATER:

Rose pours some tea into a cup. She paces a few steps, moves away from the kitchen, sits down on the couch, and sips her tea.

Jimmy, steps out in some sweat pants.

> JIMMY
>
> Are you gonna come to bed?

> ROSE
>
> I told you we need to talk.

> JIMMY
>
> And I told you I don't want to talk.

> ROSE
>
> Well, that's a problem.

> JIMMY
>
> Why? Why is there a problem? Everything's a problem anymore. The only problem is that, all of a sudden, there's always a problem.

> ROSE
>
> This is why we need to talk.

> JIMMY
>
> No. This is why we don't need to talk. All this talking lately is driving me crazy.

> ROSE
>
> This is life Jimmy.

JIMMY

No Rose, it's not, and that's what I'm saying. Life is food. Life is art. Life is having a good time and sharing moments. We've been nailing the aforementioned for almost a year now, so I ask you again, why the problems and talking all of a sudden. It's bumming me out.

ROSE

Forget it then. I don't want to bum you out.

JIMMY

What the hell is that? Don't do that.

ROSE

Life is all those things, fine, but there's other things, Jimmy.

JIMMY

Like what?

ROSE

My feelings. I have them. Maybe they get in the way of your food and your art, and whatever else, but they exist, and they need to be discussed. Not tomorrow, not next week, now. I'm not going to sleep. You don't like to talk? You just want to have a good time? This isn't a theme park. It's not a movie. It's life.

JIMMY

We obviously see things differently.

ROSE

Which I don't have a problem with.

JIMMY

Then what's the problem?

ROSE

We don't have to see eye to eye on things but at the very least we have to try and find the middle.

JIMMY

I don't do middles.

ROSE

Fine. Then I need you to pay better attention to the way I see things and find it somewhere in your heart to from time to time roll with it, or we have serious problems. Do you understand that?

JIMMY

I sat there, didn't I? I sat at that table with your entire family celebrating, what I choose to believe is the dumbest holiday of all time. You do realize the idea of sharing steroid injected turkey and marsh-mellowed sweet potatoes to commemorate the stealing of Native American land is beyond ridiculous on about ten thousand levels, yes?

ROSE

It's about spending time with family. I clearly can give a shit about the ceremony.

JIMMY

Well, I'm not really a fan of either, truth be told.

ROSE

Trust me, I understand that.

JIMMY

But I did it, didn't I?

ROSE

Begrudgingly.

JIMMY

Oh, you want I should enjoy it? It's not enough to be asked to do something you loath, but you want me to like it too? You want to talk about problems? Let's start there. Why do women always want men to do shit they don't want to do in the first place? For the record, I never want to make you do something you don't want to do.

ROSE

I appreciate that.

JIMMY

I mean it. What's with all that shit?

ROSE

All what shit?

JIMMY

I don't know. There's like this ridiculously long, seemingly endless list of shit that women regularly put men through, that for the life of us, we will never understand.

ROSE

Us? Them? We? This is beautiful. What else?

JIMMY

I'm so glad you asked.

ROSE

Not sure I can really take credit for asking, but go ahead.

JIMMY

Okay. Thank you. I got a buddy. Tony Testone. He comes home the other day to find his wife crying in the corner about some stupid holiday shit. Asks her what's up. She tells him. He says, okay babe, no sweat, I got this, I know just what to do, let me fix it. What does she do? She screams at him, kicks him in the face, breaks the poor guy's nose, and tells him to beat it. Come to find out, she didn't want a solution, she just wanted to talk. Fuck me. Talk to someone else.

ROSE

Have you lost your mind?

JIMMY

You're the one who wanted to talk.

ROSE

Is that what this is?

JIMMY

I don't know. I don't know what this is.

ROSE

I'm sorry you had to meet my family.

JIMMY

I'm sorry it didn't go the way you had hoped.

ROSE

Me too, but you know what? That's okay. Really sucks for me, but that's okay, too.

JIMMY

Your brothers and sisters studying me like I'm some sort of science project.

ROSE

They're looking out for me?

JIMMY

Looking out for you? I'm not a prowler. I'm the guy you live with.

ROSE

Who they have never met, but wait…I'm saying that's okay. We're different Jimmy. You didn't gather as a family, I did. That's fine. You don't like the holidays for specific and completely understandable reasons, that's fine too.

JIMMY

Okay stop. Right there. If that's clear, then what's the problem? We dig each other beyond, I don't know, values, ideas about life, and all that other shit, so what's the problem?

ROSE

All that other shit? Dig each other? The guy you live with? These things are the problem. And you know what? Truth be told, it's not even the words, that for the record are enough to make a person upset, but it's really what's behind them.

JIMMY

Behind? I don't think that way. Not everything has subtext. I say what I mean.

ROSE

Okay, then let's keep it simple. I woke up this morning. I rolled over, kissed your head and recited a list of things, things that you did for me, for my life over the last year, that I appreciated deeply, and was deeply grateful for.

Thankful was the word. Thankful for this, thankful for that, a long list that even included just the right amount of cream that you put into my coffee.

JIMMY

Yes. That was nice.

ROSE

You remember what you said in return?

JIMMY

Specifically?

ROSE

Thanks for everything, Rose.

JIMMY

I meant it.

ROSE

Meant what?

JIMMY

Whatever. I lumped it all together. So I'm not a wordsmith.

ROSE

You're not a small retarded boy either Jimmy, come on.

JIMMY

This is not okay.

ROSE

I agree.

JIMMY

What do you want me to say?

ROSE

Again, it's not what you say but rather how you say it. It's what you mean.

JIMMY

I just explained to you—

ROSE

Intentions Jimmy. The words we use, or don't use in this case, whether you like it or not, are informative. They point to what's next. What you intend to do when the fun stops, because contrary to the way you go about living, although charming at first, and exciting for a time, things get serious. Fun and excitement is replaced with struggle and deeper meaning. Hard pill to swallow, I know. I didn't write it, but that's the way it goes. It can be beautiful or it can be an ugly, dead thing. But that's a choice.

People pick these things. I see the potential of pretty when I look at us. What do you see?

JIMMY

Right now?

ROSE

Sure, why not?

JIMMY

I have no idea. I said. I didn't say. Maybe what I mean or meant. I have no idea. I'm confused. You want I should see something? Not sure what I'm even looking at.

ROSE

Well, take a good look. Study it, and get an idea, because this is the other part. Women are crazy? We want to talk to you sometimes? Oh my God. Solutions aren't always necessary, we just need a shoulder every once and a while? The fucking nerve.

JIMMY

I can't.

ROSE

You're gonna have to, Jimmy. Yes, we want you to enjoy our company, even in shitty situations and not have to watch you sit there like a five year old, sulking like he didn't get all the toys he wanted. We are completely insane. And yes, every once and a while we would like to hear nice things. Why? Because it makes us feel good. That's not a gal thing. It's called being a human being. But here's the real crazy part.

The part that actually separates me from the other crazies. I can live, or rather live without all that stuff, because I love you for who you are. I can accept the fact that you are basically a cripple stumbling around trying to figure out how to get from A to B without smashing into sharp objects. If I could die, go to heaven, slap the shit out of both of your parents, and then come back home, I'd buy the ticket, but unfortunately, that's not gonna be possible. So I choose to accept you for the way that you are. But what I can not accept, simply because of my will to survive and evolve, is the idea of you wasting my time.

JIMMY

Holy shit. When did I start wasting your time?

ROSE

No no no. It's not an accusation, it's a question. For the future. I'm now asking you a question.

JIMMY

I'm sorry, I seemed to have missed that part. Can you repeat the question?

ROSE

I'm asking you to try, Jimmy. Are you willing to try to be the kind of man that a woman like me, any woman for that matter, can believe in? Believe in the fact that he is willing to move forward, be a grown-up, light a giant match, set your horrific childhood on fire, and take this shit seriously. That you have yet to show me, and that is the problem. That is why I am asking you now, because I draw the line here.

JIMMY

Wait a minute. What line? Where did this line begin? I didn't know anything was wrong in the first place and now you are drawing lines?

ROSE

You didn't know anything was wrong?

JIMMY

Is there a parrot in the room? What did I just say?

ROSE

I don't know. I'm afraid I couldn't understand you because you are an idiot. Wait, before you blow up like an ape let me finish. The reason I am saying all of this is because I want to help you not be an idiot.

JIMMY

What the fuck is going on?

ROSE

I am pregnant. That is what the fuck is going on, Jimmy. I'm pregnant.

JIMMY

Okay.

ROSE

Good answer. Now, I had hoped to gather for a Thanksgiving feast with my family, and you, wishful that they would be one in the same, but later for that, for now...I had hoped to share that information with all. A joyous occasion. That clearly didn't go as planned. Here we are now. What do you think?

JIMMY

What do I think?

ROSE

Okay, I'm going to count to ten. I'm also going to do it out loud, although annoying and childish, I think it's an important sound to hear while you gather thoughts and come up with the right or potentially wrong thing to say. If you don't say something by the time I am done, I'm going to say a few things myself, that I really don't want to say, but at that point I'm afraid I will have no choice.

JIMMY

Just give me a second—

ROSE

Take ten of them. Nine, eight, seven, six, five, four, three, two...

Jimmy sits.

ROSE

I'm way too emotional and freaked out right now to be my level self. I'm not interested in raising a child alone. You're in or you're out. I'm less than a month pregnant. You understand what that means, yes?

Jimmy is frozen but manages to nod his head up and down.

ROSE

Think about it, and keep in mind, it's a much bigger thing than just yes or no... Now I'll go to bed.

She exits.

LIGHTS OUT

ACT TWO

SCENE 4

FOUR YEARS LATER:

DONNIE enters. He is topless, very muscular and seems to be oiled up a bit. He wipes himself down with a small towel, and then makes his way to the bar. He checks himself in the mirror over the bar, makes himself a drink, and flexes a few times.

Jimmy, enters.

JIMMY
Did you just shave your chest in my daughter's bathroom?

Donnie turns.

DONNIE
Yes, Jimmy I did.

Donnie turns back to the mirror to admire his work.

JIMMY
Why did you do that, Donnie?

DONNIE
Because I was prickly Jimmy, and nobody likes prickly. Looking like an ape is out. Do yourself a favor and get rid of that shit.

JIMMY
Why would you shave your chest in Zoey's sink?

DONNIE

You want I should shave my chest in your bathroom? You want my hairs in the master sink?

JIMMY

No I don't. But If I had to choose between the aforementioned destinations for chest shaving then yes, I pick the master bath over the four-year-old child's, yes. What the hell's the matter with you?

Donnie moves over to Jimmy.

DONNIE

Okay. I'm gonna need you to relax.

JIMMY

Jesus Christ. I've just asked Rose for partial custody. Last thing I need her concerned about is the pubic hair where our 4 year old daughter brushes her teeth.

DONNIE

Sit down.

JIMMY

Don't feel like it.

DONNIE

I don't need you like this.

JIMMY

Standing?

DONNIE

Don't be cute. The anxiety almost has a layer within the atmosphere here. Now sit down.

Jimmy sits.

JIMMY

Animal.

Donnie sits next to him.

DONNIE

I'll clean up the fur in Zoey's sink.

JIMMY

Thank you.

Donnie checks his watch.

DONNIE

I got these two girls coming over here. They are young, and they are pretty.

JIMMY

I have no doubt.

DONNIE

Do you trust me?

JIMMY

With most things.

DONNIE

Back to back in the alley. Do you trust me?

JIMMY

Sure I trust you.

DONNIE

Good. Now I want you to look out there.

Jimmy and Donnie look out.

DONNIE

You know what's out there?

JIMMY

The front lawn?

DONNIE

Life Jimmy. Life is out there. Just waiting for us. The good part. The part where we now know the shit we thought we knew when we were young only now we really know it. You know how powerful that is? You know how dangerous that is? I push buttons on a phone and girls show up. Young girls. Pleased as punch to be there with similar interests.

JIMMY

I get it. Zoey has a similar setup with her babysitters. Only they stay clothed. Could be the same girls. I should actually be careful.

DONNIE

Shut up. Stop thinking. Close your eyes and look.

JIMMY

Well, that's gonna be tricky, isn't it?

DONNIE

Just pick one and listen.

Jimmy keeps his eyes open.

DONNIE

Things have changed. All the struggle. The push and pull of yesterday is but a memory. We're all playing the same game now. They come over, we do what we do, and when the night ends, they get dressed and leave. Like because they want to. It's amazing. I just want you to look. That's all.

Today. Right now. Just beyond yonder. Freedom, happiness, and a general lack of ball busting no longer ends around forty, no, this is when life begins.

Jimmy stands up.

JIMMY

Sounds fantastic Donnie, but I got a kid.

DONNIE

That's no excuse.

JIMMY

Excuse for what?

DONNIE

People with kids do it all the time and just for the record it really pisses the people off who don't have any. Come to dinner. I can't I got the kid. Wanna get a drink? Can't cuz of the kid. Fun any time soon? Kid.

JIMMY

My kids not an excuse. I love Zoey very much.

DONNIE

Then show her some respect. You don't think she wants you having a good time?

JIMMY

You obviously don't understand small children. They care about nothing having to do with other people.

DONNIE

Well, that's shitty.

JIMMY

Yeah, but you love 'em anyway. A very special kind of love. And look, although we have just recently decided to part and go our separate ways, unfortunately, I still love Rose too.

DONNIE

I understand that. She's the mother of your child. How could you not?

JIMMY

It's fresh is what I'm saying. And just so we're clear, I don't need an excuse. The idea of a double date, here in this home that Rose and I shared for the last five years, forget the fact that it's with girls who just recently in life would stand up and grab their books when they hear a bell ring, that aside, for now, here, it just feels wrong.

Donnie stands.

DONNIE

I told you they got the tent at my place. Goddamn termites everywhere. You wanna go there? Let's go. I think it's probably a health risk, but that's what I'm willing to do for this situation because I really think you need it.

JIMMY

I appreciate the commitment. I really do.

DONNIE

Back to back.

Jimmy sits back down.

JIMMY

It's not just the location.

DONNIE

You want I should find some old broads? That's possible too. Anything's possible these days. Why the hell we would choose to do that is beyond me given the options, but again, if that's what makes you feel comfortable.

Donnie sits down with him.

JIMMY

Are you listening to me? The whole thing is starting to make me feel uncomfortable and that's what I'm saying.

Jimmy stands up and moves for the kitchen. Donnie follows.

DONNIE

Do you not remember the conversation we had? I know it was a while back but I remember it like a childhood beating.

JIMMY

I remember.

DONNIE

Did you not watch me? Did you not see me waste years of my life? Take your own advice for the love of God. Don't listen to me, don't listen to your parents, the dopey fucks, rest in peace, but Jesus Christ, listen to yourself. You watched them. You watched me. I mean at least I made it out alive; but for what? So that now I can watch you? Come on.

JIMMY

Not every situation is the same, Donnie.

DONNIE

Hey. One guy takes a boat, gets nipped on by a few sharks and almost drowns, the other guy takes a plane and naps, they both end up at the fuckin' event. You dig?

JIMMY

No, I do not dig. That's ridiculous. The way we deal with our own personal and very different set of circumstances should vary. Everyone's different. You can't just throw it all together like that. Different is different. I like rice, she likes potatoes. She's late, I hate late people. Christmas, and fuckin' Christmas trees? I'm a Jew. We're different people. You want us to live together? How? Difference is a motherfucker, man.

DONNIE

Okay, I don't even know what the hell we're talking about anymore. I just want you to have a good time tonight. That's all.

JIMMY

I'm dying for a good time. You kidding me.

DONNIE

You think I joke when it comes to time? I'm the last guy to do that. I'm twenty, seven minutes ago.

JIMMY

I'm right there with you, pal. Unfortunately, I'm just not so clear on what's what right this second. I'm all jammed up. You think I want to be arguing with you about this? You think I'm happy being mentally torn between sitting alone in a room obsessing over conversations pertaining to window locks and air purifiers, as opposed to having sex with young people who also have nice skin?

DONNIE

No brainer.

JIMMY

You'd think so wouldn't you?

DONNIE

I would, yes.

JIMMY

Well? Naked pre-aged bodies versus daily arguments over nothing is all-consuming at this point. Seemingly ridiculous discrepancies about where the crib does or does not go, or why we need to investigate preschools like it's even possible four-year-old gatherings could potentially end in violence or death. I'm trying to figure out how two people ended up wanting to kill each other because one of 'em couldn't see that it's completely impossible for a baby to swallow a baseball. These are the things that ended my not marriage, and that's what's pumping through my head right now. You want me to talk shop with a twenty-year-old girl who for all I know still wipes back to front? Come on.

Jimmy moves for the couch and sits back down.

DONNIE

Okay.

JIMMY

Okay?

DONNIE

I'm just trying to help.

JIMMY

I understand that. I appreciate that. All I'm trying to say is that I'm afraid, maybe, my head's not in the right place. Just yet. Not today.

Donnie pulls out his phone, and pretends to look for a contact.

JIMMY

What are you doing?

DONNIE

I'm gonna call the really pretty, young, sexy girls who just want to have fun with us and take our minds off of whatever stressors might be weighing us down at this very moment… And cancel.

Jimmy moves to stand. Donnie pushes him back into his seat.

DONNIE

No, no, no. Stay seated. Right there. Don't get up. Do like I did, and then call me in a few years when you figure it out.

JIMMY

Don't do this.

Donnie puts the phone back into his pocket.

DONNIE

You trust me?

JIMMY

We been over this.

DONNIE

Then stand up. The pain's a bitch, but you gotta push through that last rep. You want abs? Do the crunches. You wanna flex, look in the mirror, and see a middle-aged Navy Seal? Do the goddamn work. That's it.

Donnie sits back down next to Jimmy.

DONNIE

I wasted too many years, Jimmy. Almost a nickel. Half a decade I made sick noises over this rotten piece of shit. Why? Because I thought I was supposed to be with her. Who said so? The world? It's bullshit. Don't do it.

JIMMY

Again, and all do respect, but our relationships ended because of completely—

DONNIE

I know, I know. Different, difference, different! Potatoes and rice. Different boats. I know. Same lake though. Or maybe the lake's what's different and the boats the common denominator. Either way we are in this together, and I'm telling you, now I know. We're plain just better off this way. I've seen both sides, It's a science project, and I now have the results. You wanna get into semantics of how we got there?

This one cheated, that one shut down, the other one started wearing men's clothes, it don't make a difference.

JIMMY

I was gonna ask you about that. You heard about Tony Testone's wife?

DONNIE

Unreal.

JIMMY

She grabs herself like she's got a penis now.

DONNIE

You saw her?

JIMMY

Him. I saw him. There's no her left. Remember that pretty voice? She sounds like Tom Waits now.

DONNIE

Makes me sick.

JIMMY

Hey. To each their own.

DONNIE

No, I don't gotta problem with it. She, or he, or whatever wants to watch ball games and eat peanuts, great. Tony, I'm saying. He's sick over it. Therapy three times a week and antidepressants like jelly beans.

JIMMY

You can imagine one day your wife decides to become a man, that might be rough.

DONNIE

Ruff? Ruff is right, but surely an excuse to move on guilt-free. No regrets. That's what I'm saying.

JIMMY

I think you might be underestimating the power of trauma.

DONNIE

Bullshit. What trauma? We're adults. Trauma happens early. Anything after twenty is clinically classified injury. You fall down, skin your knee, get up and keep playing.

JIMMY

Wow. You're good. Do I have to pay for this?

DONNIE

You should be so lucky to have the option of trading curren-cy for knowledge over pain and time.

JIMMY

That's pretty.

DONNIE

Listen to me.

JIMMY

I don't want to anymore. I'm done. I don't wanna think, I been thinking for a week straight with no breaks, and I don't wanna listen either. I'm in. If for no other reason than to get you to shut the fuck up, I'm in. Okay?

DONNIE

Fantastic. I'll take it.

Jimmy stands up.

JIMMY

I'm not shaving my chest.

Donnie stands.

DONNIE

That's fine.

JIMMY

And I'm not taking Mary or Molly or whatever the hell it's called, either.

DONNIE

We'll see.

JIMMY

What time?

Donnie looks at his watch.

DONNIE

Girls should be here in an hour, so probably two.

JIMMY

What does that mean?

DONNIE

Being on time's very ten years ago.

JIMMY

Great. I'm already exhausted.

LIGHTS OUT.

SCENE 5

Distant moaning and various sex sounds are heard off stage.

BINKI is alone on stage with Jimmy. They sit on opposite ends of the couch. She keeps one eye on Jimmy, and the other on her phone as she scrolls through some social media page.

> JIMMY

Anything good over there?

She takes one last look and then puts the phone down on the table.

> BINKI

So what's up? You married?

> JIMMY

No. No I'm not.

> BINKI

You sure about that?

> JIMMY

Pretty positive, yeah. Why? You?

> BINKI

No, I'm not married.

> JIMMY

I was kidding.

> BINKI

You're very funny. Girlfriend?

> JIMMY

What?

She point at him.

                    BINKI
Serious girlfriend?

                    JIMMY
No, I don't have a girlfriend.

                    BINKI
Not seeing someone you dig or whatever?

                    JIMMY
Definitely not, no. What kind of a name is Binki?

                    BINKI
I don't know. What kind of a name is Jimmy?

                    JIMMY
Fair enough, but Binki isn't really a common -

                    BINKI
Who gives a shit about my name? What are you gay?

                    JIMMY
Because I'm interested in your name?

                    BINKI
Now that you say it, it does seem like something a gay guy
would be interested in, but no. Are you?

                    JIMMY
I am not.

                    BINKI
And you're not dating a woman?

                    JIMMY
Not presently no. Why do you keep asking me that?

BINKI

The same reason I asked if you're gay, because we've been here in this room alone for over twenty minutes and you haven't tried to fuck me.

JIMMY

Wow.

BINKI

Right?

JIMMY

Is that what usually happens in the first twenty minutes.

BINKI

Twenty minutes of what Jimmy? What the fuck are you talking about?

JIMMY

You just…

BINKI

What?

JIMMY

I'm confused.

BINKI

I know you find me attractive. You seem okay. What's the issue?

JIMMY

Why are you like this?

Binki gets up.

                          BINKI

Oh, Jesus Christ.

Jimmy stands.

                          JIMMY

Wait a minute.

                          BINKI

Like what? This should be great.

                          JIMMY

I'm just saying. That's how it goes? Most men alone in a room
with you are trying to fuck you?

                          BINKI

Unless they're gay, pretty much, yeah. Either that or they're
thinking about it.

                          JIMMY

That's nice you think so highly of yourself.

                          BINKI

Oh come on dude, wake up.

                          JIMMY

Really?

                          BINKI

Really what? I'm half your age, my friend Monica is in the
other room having sex with your buddy. Everyone's high.
Come on. What am I doing here? Is this a date?

                          JIMMY

Half my age?

BINKI

You wanna do the math? I'm sure I'm not far off.

                    JIMMY

So that's it? You're just here for sex?

                    BINKI

It's surely not for the stimulating conversation, Joey.

                    JIMMY

It's still Jimmy, and again, why are you like this?

                    BINKI

Say that again, and I'll punch you in the dick.

                    JIMMY

Okay. I don't want to have sex with you.

                    BINKI

I'm crushed.

                    JIMMY

Can't we just talk?

                    BINKI

Oh God.

                    JIMMY

I mean it.

Binki moves for the bar.

                    BINKI

I'm way too sober for this.

She makes a drink.

JIMMY

Didn't you take that Molly too or whatever?

BINKI

I'm allergic to Methylone.

JIMMY

What's…never mind.

BINKI

What do you wanna know Jimmy? I'm three seconds from calling an Uber. It's Friday night. What the fuck?

JIMMY

You really came here with the intention of sleeping with me?

BINKI

I was very open to the idea, yes.

JIMMY

Why?

BINKI

Monica said she hooked up with a sexy older dude, and that he had a cute friend, showed me a picture of you, and I said cool.

JIMMY

That's it? Just a picture?

BINKI

No, I also asked what your favorite color was.

JIMMY

What if I was a crazy person? Or a kidnapper? What if I had diseases?

> BINKI

Are you a hundred?

> JIMMY

I'm serious.

> BINKI

So am I.

> JIMMY

Do you have a thing for older guys?

> BINKI

Nope.

> JIMMY

Daddy issues?

> BINKI

You're so stupid.

> JIMMY

I'm perplexed.

> BINKI

Okay, let me ask you a question. Back in the forties when you were my age—

> JIMMY

Fuck you.

> BINKI

Seventies, eighties, whatever.

> JIMMY

I'm not that old.

BINKI

You're not that young either, but let me get to the point. When you were my age—

JIMMY

Nineties. Late nineties. Very late.

BINKI

Fine. Way back then, just a guess, you don't even have to be close, how many random girls you think you slept with?

JIMMY

I don't know.

BINKI

Okay. I'll do you one better. You ever sleep with a girl the night you met her and then never saw her again? If you lie you're useless.

JIMMY

Yes.

BINKI

More than once?

JIMMY

Sure.

BINKI

How 'bout this? And once again, if you can't be honest, you suck. Period. As a human being. A straight up sucky person.

JIMMY

I got it.

BINKI

Would it be safe to say that there was a time in your life when your main focus was to go out, find, and then sleep with as many girls as you possibly could? Did you place bets with friends? Did you lose count at some point? Did you buy condoms in bulk?

JIMMY

That's a lot of different questions.

BINKI

I know. And you don't have to answer any of them. You're handsome. I assume you used to be charming. You're successful, unless you come from money, either way, you had a good old time at some stage. Am I wrong?

JIMMY

No you are not.

BINKI

That's right. So what card of mine would you like to pull that I didn't just shuffle straight back into your face?

Jimmy is frozen.

BINKI

Look, I'm not sure what kind of drama you're presently going through, I can only assume it's what people like my aunties and uncles refer to as mid-life crisis, but let me give you a piece of advice that might help, as you claw your way back into the modern world. Things have changed a bit. Me Too doesn't just mean we'd like an equal paycheck or that we won't be pushed around. It also means, we too, like to have fun, sometimes that fun involves Penis. Don't judge me. It's gross.

JIMMY

Why are you like this?

She punches him in the dick. He barrels over.

JIMMY

Oh, God. Why?

BINKI

I warned you.

Jimmy slinks down onto the floor and whimpers, as he begins his slow crawl toward the couch.

BINKI

Oh, come on. It can't be that bad.

Jimmy slides up onto the couch.

JIMMY

You ever think that maybe the reason someone wouldn't want to sleep with you is because for some reason or another they actually don't find you attractive?

BINKI

Yeah, sure. Some people but not you. You got issues, but not being attracted to me isn't one of them.

JIMMY

I'm sad.

BINKI

I can see that?

JIMMY

I'm sorry.

BINKI

Don't be sorry to me.

JIMMY

Well, who should I be sorry to Binki? Binki? What kind of a name... You know what? I know you think you have me all figured out, but you don't. And I'm not judging you. You wanna have sex with a bunch of dudes, go right ahead.

BINKI

Thanks dad.

JIMMY

God, that scares me on so many different levels, you have no idea.

BINKI

Whatever.

JIMMY

You know, I'm not really sure why I feel the need to explain anything to you at this point in our relationship but I'm going to do it any way.

BINKI

Edge of my seat.

JIMMY

Here's why I don't want to sleep with you?

BINKI

Cool, but for the record that door has officially closed.

JIMMY

I'll get over it.

BINKI

I don't know. I'm a three door kinda gal.

JIMMY

What?

BINKI

I'm kidding.

JIMMY

The reason I don't want to sleep with you has nothing to do with you, so I guess you're right. You see, it's sex in general. The act itself has become this distant memory that may or may not have ever been a steady part of my life. I can't even remember the last time I had it, and I've only been single for like two weeks. You know, I used to think that what I did with my body was a gift.

BINKI

Oh boy.

JIMMY

Yeah, well maybe you're right. But in any case, that's what I thought and that's all that mattered. That's the point. All of a sudden, it was like I'm sitting around waiting.

Like I'm at a deli with a shitty paper ticket. You know what that can do to a man's ego? A man like me?

BINKI

What are you talking about?

JIMMY

I'm having a rough time.

BINKI

I can see that.

JIMMY

Yes. There's someone else.

BINKI

You mean I'm not the only one?

JIMMY

Can you just stop being a smart-ass for like ten seconds? I get it. You're young and sharp and female, and you're not to be jacked with. Noted. I'm begging you, give it just the smallest break. Please. I'm this close to melting right now. I can feel it.

BINKI

Well, don't do that.

JIMMY

Do you have any idea what I come from?

BINKI

This is gonna get fuckin' deep isn't it.

Binki slides on a pair of sunglasses.

JIMMY

I come from hell. Literal hell. I should be robbing houses. Or serial killing. Or something really terrible.

BINKI

We all have our shit.

JIMMY

Mine stinks.

BINKI

That's the thing about shit.

                              JIMMY

Correct, but guess what?

                              BINKI

Chicken butt.

                              JIMMY

I changed.

                              BINKI

Good for you.

                              JIMMY

I made a decision. I busted my ass and did the work. Why?
Because I met a woman who made me wanna do that shit.
I even went to see a doctor. Fucking guy with a beard and
everything.

                              BINKI

Yeah? How'd that work out for you?

                              JIMMY

Honestly? It was beautiful. For the first time in my life it all
seemed like something really good was gonna happen. Baby,
wife, house. The whole trip. And that's no small leap for a guy
like me. A woman tells you she's pregnant, and you come from
my house, trust me, you're looking for the closest window.

                              BINKI

So dramatic.

                              JIMMY

I can't wait till you're a grown up and some real shit happens
to you.

BINKI

Whatever. So what? You didn't plunge to your death, you manned up and married the broad. Big deal.

JIMMY

No. We never got married. To her credit she understood my fear about that part and waved it. All she cared about was that I showed up. And that's exactly what I did.

BINKI

And?

JIMMY

And we did pregnant. One of the best nine months of my life if I'm being honest.

BINKI

And then?

JIMMY

And then the kid came out and she lost her fucking mind.

BINKI

I'm sure she did. What kind you have?

JIMMY

Girl kind?

BINKI

Of course.

JIMMY

You know what? You don't know everything.

BINKI

I know more than you think I know.

JIMMY

See. That right there. That's a problem. And again, I don't care who you sleep with or what kind of drugs you do or do not take do to allergies, or whatever, but I'm telling you, you don't know everything. Like it or not, you age, your brain grows, and I'm just saying you should be open to that kinda shit, because the second you think you have it all figured out is the same second some twenty year old punches you in the dick.

BINKI

Thanks for the advice. And I thought I was just coming over here for some mediocre sex.

JIMMY

You don't stop do you?

BINKI

No, but let me just make sure I'm clear here before I dig in. You want credit is that it?

JIMMY

Credit for what?

BINKI

You stepped up for this chick, decided to be a man and a father, and what? You want magic? Did you imagine rainbows shooting out of vagina and rolling green fields of laughing children? I mean, what are you an idiot?

JIMMY

I haven't even gotten to it yet.

BINKI

Well, then get to it, and fast, because so far, if this movie was playing on a plane, I'd walk out.

JIMMY

We had something.

BINKI

Oh God.

JIMMY

Something very special that I had previously reserved for friends. Male ones. Back to back in an alley. It means, I got you. When the shit goes down, and fifty dudes come rushing down the street, I got you and you got me. Back to back in the alley.

BINKI

That's stupid.

JIMMY

Whatever.

BINKI

What kind of dumb shit do you have to do that ends with fifty dudes chasing you into an alley?

JIMMY

It's called a metaphor.

BINKI

It's a stupid metaphor.

JIMMY

Great. Fine. More to support the fact that it should have stayed reserved for men only.

BINKI

I'm sure your ex won't miss that doozy.

                              JIMMY

You're missing the point.

                              BINKI

No, I get the point. You had each others backs?

                              JIMMY

Correct. Then all of a sudden, just like that, everything changed and things were different.

                              BINKI

You mean she had a baby, and things were different? I'm shocked.

                              JIMMY

Okay, I expected different. I expected some change. I didn't expect to no longer be relevant.

                              BINKI

Do you want me to throw up all over the place? Are you even a real person?

                              JIMMY

I'm sorry, but that's just what happens. Fact. A child arrives, a man basically becomes irrelevant.

                              BINKI

Okay, I got an idea. Grow tits and produce a super food for babies with your stomach and then we can rehash this brilliant rhetoric.

                              JIMMY

Do you have children somehow?

                              BINKI

No. But my sister has four. Can't stand the whole lot, including my sister, but at the very least I see the struggle and have a deep respect for the woman's efforts.

JIMMY

As do I, but that being said and pretty much universally understood; what the hell am I supposed to do with the whole thing? You know how many books there are for new mothers? Countless. It never ends. I know this because I paid for them all. On the flip side, you know how many there are for men? One book. It's called *Talking to Crazy*. Read it cover to cover and the only thing I took away from the petite novella was this. A mother's behavior, minus the child, would be classified clinically, important adverb there, clinically, insane. Be me, and do something with that.

BINKI

Not interested.

JIMMY

What?

BINKI

In being you or doing something about it. Two problems you can keep. But what I will do, before I leave here in just a sec, is give you my thoughts.

JIMMY

This should be rich.

BINKI

Shut up.

JIMMY

Okay.

BINKI

Do you know what I have to do every day?

JIMMY

Take the morning after pill?

BINKI

Funny. No. Let's go ahead and broaden the scope for the sake of clarity. What does everyone have to do everyday? Have to. Basics only.

JIMMY

Is this a trick question?

BINKI

Sadly it might be for you.

JIMMY

What? Fuck.

BINKI

I. We. Regular people, hold for the ones that have just recently pressed a human being out of their vaginas, what do we have to do? We have to eat, and we have to sleep. That's it. Can you imagine what it's like when all of a sudden, those things become secondary. And if you say the word nature, you're an asshole.

JIMMY

Kinda got me in a pickle there?

BINKI

Do you have any idea what a woman goes through when she has a child?

JIMMY

Not physically obviously, but I was there.

BINKI

No. Not the actual birth. But bravo. After that part.

JIMMY

Yes. Yes, I do. That's what I'm talking about. I have every idea. I watched it like a show for almost five years. Felt like a life time.

BINKI

Five years?

JIMMY

That's right.

BINKI

That's not a lifetime. It's a David Bowie song. Five years?

JIMMY

Don't short me on five years. Five years is a long time. That's almost half your life.

BINKI

It's not even a percentage of yours. It's like a season, if you think about it.

JIMMY

Look, all I'm saying is that I stepped up. I don't want credit. I don't want a prize. I don't even want a pat on the back. I just want what I signed up for. At least some of it anyway. I get it, being a mother is one of the hardest jobs on the planet, but if I can't help, or if I feel I'm just in the way all the time, what am I supposed to do?

BINKI

Get out of the way?

JIMMY

That's what I did.

                    BINKI

Literally?

                    JIMMY

Yes. Literally.

                    BINKI

Jesus Christ.

                    JIMMY

I couldn't take it anymore.

                    BINKI

You couldn't take what anymore?

                    JIMMY

Feeling useless. Feeling like I had no place. Feeling like the only reason I was around was to pick up the check.

                    BINKI

Someone's gotta do it.

                    JIMMY

Fine. I figured I could do that just as easily from across the street. My daughter, who just for the record remains out of this conversation, do to the fact that she means the world to me, and has no place anywhere within the fuckery of my brain during all of this, but she certainly wasn't getting the prime experience of good together parenting.

                    BINKI

So, you bailed.

                    JIMMY

Something like that, yeah.

                              BINKI

You know why?

                              JIMMY

Because I was losing it.

                              BINKI

Nope. Because you're a pussy.

                              JIMMY

Great.

                              BINKI

And I hate that word but I save it for very special people.

                              JIMMY

I'm honored.

                              BINKI

You shouldn't be. You're a pussy because all you did was accept whatever "hell" you came from, which I'm absolutely
positive couldn't have been that bad, but even if it was, once
again, you're still a pussy, because rather than stick it out and
make it through the rough, you decided to pout and just rot
in the muck you were raised in.

All that talk about stepping up and making decisions. The
only decision you made was to walk away from the right
thing to do?

                              JIMMY

Look, it—

                              BINKI

I'm not done. You can bitch shortly. This way I can pretend
to listen while waiting for a car, and not feel the need to reply.

JIMMY

You're special.

BINKI

True, but not nearly as much so as the kind of woman that had the nerve to deal with your shit, allow you to place that damaged sperm into her body, and all the while not demand a ring and papers. She's some kind of gem. Had you stuck it out? You wanna talk about a prize? How 'bout a woman who's proud to have a man that did that for her? Through all the shit and insanity it is to raise a small person, a girl no less, on this backward fucked-up planet, to have someone be there through thick and thin? Right about the time you bailed, is right about the same time you should have been ass to back in the alley. Or whatever that stupid shit was called.

JIMMY

I'm really glad we had this talk.

BINKI

The problem is you don't understand women. Maybe had you tried a little harder to do so, you would have realized that the whole purpose of change and growth is what the general evolution process is all about.

JIMMY

Who the fuck are you?

BINKI

Binki. Brenda was my given name, I choose not to use it.

Donnie, storms onto stage soaking wet with sweat. He wears nothing but a towel wrapped around his waist.

DONNIE

I think I killed Monica.

Binki immediately moves for the door and exits. Donnie turns to Jimmy.

DONNIE

Don't leave me out here alone.

JIMMY

What do you mean you think you killed Monica?

DONNIE

I don't know dude, I'm freaking out.

JIMMY

Okay, well, do I need to call an ambulance?

DONNIE

You can't do that. Girls popping Molly's like skittles all night, I'm not even sure how old she is, I'm forty something, this is no good.

JIMMY

Jesus Christ.

Jimmy moves, but Donnie jumps in front of the door with his hands up.

DONNIE

Wait.

JIMMY

Wait for what?

DONNIE

Please don't go in there.

JIMMY

Did you hurt her?

                    DONNIE

Well if she's fucking dead the answer is pretty much yes,
don't you think?

A bang on the door.

                    DONNIE

AHHH!

*Donnie jumps out of the way. The door swings open. Binki
sticks her head out.*

                    BINKI

No one comes in here. I need coffee grounds, rubbing alco-
hol, a steak knife, and some Band-Aids.

                    DONNIE

She's alive?

                    BINKI

We're not in the clear yet.

                    JIMMY

Coffee grounds?

                    BINKI

Hurry the fuck up.

*Jimmy darts for the kitchen and starts to gather items. Donnie
starts to pace.*

                    DONNIE

I'm joining the church, or the farm, or some other place.
This is so bad.

                    BINKI

Just relax.

DONNIE

How old is she?

BINKI

Relax dude.

DONNIE

That's no answer.

BINKI

Not old enough to die, if that's what you mean.

DONNIE

That's not what I meant…and don't say that.

Jimmy storms back over with a small bucket full of items.

JIMMY

Yes or no, do I need to call an ambulance?

BINKI

No way, dude. She's only seventeen.

DONNIE

Oh, fuck me.

BINKI

I'm kidding. [To Jimmy] No, not yet. I got this. Just chill out.
Good vibes only. Got it?

JIMMY

Got it.

Binki exits with the bucket.

DONNIE

Never again. Never ever. That's it. I swear to God that was it.

                    JIMMY

What the hell happened?

                    DONNIE

I'm feeling some kinda way right now. This is some special
shit I'm telling you.

                    JIMMY

What happened?

                    DONNIE

I'm telling you.

                    JIMMY

Tell me!

Donnie slams back the drink.

                    DONNIE

Okay, so we're in there. I mean we pretty much got right to
it. Started with some lotion and some petting and what have
you, but very quickly, next thing you know, we're going at it.
And it was fucking great at first. Pretty much outstanding
as far as these things go, you know? I don't know if it was
the drugs, or her, or both, but it was pretty fucking amazing.
I mean it felt like I was doing the right thing. You know how
it feels when it just fits?

Jimmy checks the door.

                    DONNIE

Well, It just did. It's like we were dancing together like we'd
practiced all along.

                    JIMMY

What the hell are you talking about?

DONNIE

I'm saying, like if it was a dance or something, we'd practiced it. Like it was something well-rehearsed, but not like forced or for show or whatever... It was just great. Really great.

JIMMY

So what happened?

DONNIE

So, I'm on top. You know on top?

JIMMY

It's been a while, but yes, I know on top.

DONNIE

So there I am, and I'm doing my thing. And I know it was working out because...well, because of two things actually. You know you got that little mirror over on the dresser?

JIMMY

Sure.

DONNIE

Well, I could kind of see myself, or just a good piece of my arm, and you know when you get that pump after a good set of curls or skull crushers or whatever?

JIMMY

Go ahead.

DONNIE

Whatever. I knew it was good because I felt good, and I looked good, and you feel good you look good. I mean if you look good you feel good. Whatever. It and I both felt good is what I'm saying. And the other thing was that she was really into it because her eyes started to do this thing like roll back a bit and in these circles she was making with them. Whatever. I could just tell it was going right. So, her eyes were doing that thing, and I was trying real hard to focus, cause at first I kinda liked it, but then it started to look kinda weird, but I didn't wanna loose my concentration, so I just started going and going, like pretty hard, right?

JIMMY

Right.

DONNIE

And then I must have been focussing too much or something because all of a sudden her face started to go blurry, but again, I didn't wanna loose what I had going, and I didn't want my rhythm to get all screwed up, so I just kept staring at her and driving and pushing, and just doing my thing. Too much now at this point because all of a sudden, I got lost. Then the craziest shit started happening. Like in flashes, in perfect sequence, every woman I had ever been with, sexually, started to show up on Monica's face. Right there looking back up at me. Like this sick and vivid mirage of montaged faces. I mean all the way back to the seventh grade. Jillian Gray. Ashley Mallory. Tammy Brookstone. Guadalupe Godinez —

JIMMY

I got it.

DONNIE

You got it. Perfect order, an order I couldn't make consciously if you paid me all the money on the earth, but there they all were. Popping up one at a time. All of 'em just looking up at me, smiling and egging me on. Needless to say I'm getting a little freaked out, on one hand sure, but on the other hand I'm kinda digging it, like in a sick twisted kinda way, cuz what the hell, I'm only human and this is pretty kinky and weird. But before I could slow down and regain some sort of sexy pace back, shit turned real dark real quick. I mean, right when I started getting into the groove of all these changing faces, the sequence stopped and froze. And just like that, there it was. Lily's crooked Albanian face staring right up at me. Winking and shit. Now this was certainly not a face I was happy to see. So I start driving in, even harder now, cuz now I just wanna kill the bitch, like fuck her right out of my head, out of Monica's head, right out of the fucking room or something, ya know? The harder I pumped the more she'd fade, so goddamn it, I kept to pumping. And I feel horrible saying it now, and I'll deny it if you ever bring it up socially, but in that moment, I just wanted 'em all to die. I was so confused, and I didn't know what else to do, so I just kept pounding away like a murderer and didn't stop till all I could see was Monica's angelic pretty little face right back where it belonged. And when she finally came back into focus, like reality, that's when I realized she was, at that point what I considered to be, very much dead. She wasn't moving, and I'm pretty sure she wasn't breathing either. So I jumped up, grabbed a towel and went running. And here we are.

Jimmy plops down into the couch.

DONNIE

Can you actually fuck someone to death?

JIMMY

I really don't know.

DONNIE

Well, if it's possible, I'm telling you I just did it. And I swear to God what I said before wasn't bullshit. I'm done. If she lives or dies, jail or freedom, that's it. I know a sign when I see one, and that's it. New leaf my boy. New leaf for sure.

Jimmy slowly nods his head.

DONNIE
So that's pretty much it for me. What have you been doing?

JIMMY
This is something. This is really something.

DONNIE
You okay?

JIMMY
I don't know. I really don't know.

Donnie sits down next to him.

DONNIE
This world's crazy man. I'm telling you. Not to mention this new power I've found. It has to be put to better use somehow. For something else I'm thinking.

JIMMY
I hope it all works out.

DONNIE
Were you saying something?

JIMMY
I don't want to live like this anymore.

DONNIE
You? Did you listen to what I just said?

JIMMY
Yeah I did. And it helped somehow.

DONNIE

Oh good.

JIMMY

What the hell am I doing here?

Binki steps back out. Jimmy and Donnie both stand. She moves slow.

Binki

Bad news, you guys…I'm kidding. She's totally fine.

DONNIE

Oh, thank God.

BINKI

She said she had a blast.

Donnie moves over and gives her a hug. His towel drops to the floor exposing his naked tush.

BINKI

Dude, seriously.

Donnie won't let go. He slowly pets her hair like she's some kind of furry animal.

BINKI

DUDE!

JIMMY

Thank you…for everything.

BINKI

Ah huh.

MONICA, early twenties, black eye make up all over her face, and drenched in sweat, steps out wearing nothing but the vin-

tage Harley shirt.

MONICA

Man, that shit was crazy.

She takes in the weird visual of naked Donnie, then turns to Jimmy.

MONICA

You got any pot?

JIMMY

I'm sorry, I know you've been through a lot, but you're gonna have to take that shirt off.

Monica takes the shirt off, exposing her naked body, and hands it over to Jimmy. He takes it.

JIMMY

I didn't mean right this second, but thank you.

LIGHTS OUT

ACT THREE

SCENE 6

TWO YEARS LATER:

Rose stands alone on stage. Her hair is shorter. She takes in the room.

Jimmy enters from the bedroom door, up left, with a small pink backpack. He looks around.

JIMMY

Hey.

ROSE

Hey.

JIMMY

Where's the child? Is she hiding?

ROSE

She's on the swing in the front yard.

JIMMY

On the swing in the front yard. All by herself on the swing.

ROSE

Big girl.

JIMMY

I can't believe she's six.

                    ROSE
That makes you pretty old doesn't it.

                    JIMMY
Even makes you old.

                    ROSE
No. I'll never get old. To you I'll always be twenty-something
and perfect.

                    JIMMY
That's unfortunately very true.

Jimmy forces a smile and holds the bag up.

                    ROSE
We'll see you next Friday.

Rose takes the bag and heads for the door. Jimmy follows

                    JIMMY
You know, this weekend I caught myself just watching her.
Thinking about you…and me—

                    ROSE
I'll see you next week, Jimmy.

                    JIMMY
Wait. Relax.

Rose waits at the door.

                    JIMMY
I was thinking, I just hope I had at least a little something to
do with why she's so intelligent and cool.

Rose smiles.

JIMMY

Is that a smile, like you wonder the same, or like sure ya did champ?

ROSE

You're a good father.

JIMMY

Well, had I relied on my own instincts she might be out there knifing tires, so thank you for the guidance.

ROSE

Did I tell you last week she told me she needed space?

JIMMY

Wow. No. What did you say?

ROSE

Truth of the matter is, I've been dying for some free time, and now that I have it I have no clue what to do with it… So, I told her to fuck off.

JIMMY

Good. Very good. Strong.

ROSE

Love of my life, but trust me, when no one's looking, I scream into a pillow.

JIMMY

That's kinda hot.

ROSE

You're an idiot.

JIMMY

Absolutely.

They stare at each other in silence for a bit.

ROSE

Thank you.

JIMMY

For being an idiot?

ROSE

No. Thank you for making the right decision seven years ago. I'm not really sure, nor will I ever understand all that happened after, but if it was all for that one moment, then I owe you that. So thank you.

Jimmy nods.

JIMMY

Look, if you ever need help filling that new free time you have, I'd be happy to—

ROSE

That's not what I was saying.

JIMMY

Okay. Sorry.

ROSE

See you next week?

Jimmy nods his head. Rose moves for the door again.

JIMMY

Wait.

She stops.

ROSE

What?

JIMMY

I just—

ROSE

You don't have to say anything.

JIMMY

I want to.

ROSE

Fine. Then say it. But I don't want to be uncomfortable every time we do this.

JIMMY

I'm not trying to do that. I get confused. You say things. I'm not so sure what they mean.

ROSE

I just say things. Not everything needs an answer.

JIMMY

Some things do.

ROSE

Zoey's outside.

JIMMY

She's a big girl on the swing. She needs her space. She's fine.

Rose drops the bag and storms back into the living room.

ROSE

What? Say something. I can't do this every time I come here to pick her up.

JIMMY

You think I like it?

ROSE

What do you want?

JIMMY

Come on Rose. You don't know what I want?

ROSE

What do want that you can actually have? And that's on you.
I'm not being mean.

JIMMY

I don't know. Maybe just to understand you. Have you understand me. Is that so difficult? Maybe if we can get there,
we could both get what we want, or something like it.

ROSE

Jimmy.

JIMMY

What? We talk, I feel like a crazy person half the time.

ROSE

You still in therapy?

JIMMY

No. Are you?

ROSE

Goddamn right I am. You should know, you're paying for it.

JIMMY

I'm gonna go back. I just needed a break. I have strategy, it's
not like I'm thoughtless.

ROSE

Strategy, huh?

JIMMY

Think about it. You send a narcissist to go talk about himself a couple times a week to a person who doesn't share back and you want results? Who's the idiot there?

ROSE

You're not a narcissist.

JIMMY

No?

ROSE

Not clinically.

JIMMY

Anyway, the real reason I'm taking a break is that I caught the guy I had been seeing regularly, do what I thought was some texting. I was mid breakdown about some horrible childhood moment I was reliving, I look up and this jack off's glued to his phone. Guy's on some dating app, swiping away while I'm trying to figure out why I'm forty-something and still single.

So, then I started seeing a woman therapist of all things, which at first seemed like the right move, but then all we ever talked about was the difference between men and women and how truly difficult, if not impossible, it is, to really hear and deeply understand each other.

So, I was like, really, then what the hell am I doing here with you? Apparently, you can't even hear me. What? It's different because you're a doctor? You're not immune to the human action or emotion of processing, are you? Just because you have a degree? What the hell is that? Anyway, needless to say we hit a little bump, and I decided to take a little break.

ROSE

Yeah, I think maybe you do deserve a little break.

JIMMY

I just want to be honest with you, Rose. That's it. That's all I have. I want to be honest, tell you how I feel, and have it be okay.

ROSE

You think I have a problem with that?

JIMMY

I don't know. I haven't asked recently.

ROSE

I don't have a problem with you being honest, as long as that's all it is.

JIMMY

See. I don't know what that means.

ROSE

Nothing needs to be explained, Jimmy.

JIMMY

I say it does.

ROSE

Okay. For who?

JIMMY

What?

ROSE

Jesus Christ! For who? For you? For me? We all got our own shit, Jimmy. I have a hard-enough time trying to figure out how I feel half the time. It's hard enough being honest with myself, let alone helping you do the shit. Say what you gotta say, but leave me out of it. Or don't. Just pick one because this is driving me crazy too.

JIMMY

I just wanna tell you the truth.

ROSE

Fucking do it then.

JIMMY

Fine. I woke up one day and somehow came to the realization that the people I chose to share my world with, even the ones that came out of my body, were making me crazy and ruining my life. Hit me pretty hard. So hard that it almost made me forget about how life used to be. The fear, the loneliness, the moments staring at blank walls wondering what the hell it's all for anyway. Then I realized that all sucked too, then further realized that life just sucks period, and at the end of the day, all we have, all we really need, are the people we chose to share it with to give all that struggle and torture meaning. Somehow it ends up beautiful.

Jimmy moves to her.

JIMMY

I'm sorry it took me so long to catch up, but I love you, I love Zoey, and I'm sorry I didn't hang in there when I should have. You deserved better. But I'm okay knowing that, and I'm okay dealing with the consequences of my own stupidity, as long as we get to continue doing what we're doing with that little girl out there. I fuck that up, and I promise you'll find me looking for a tall bridge somewhere.

                    ROSE

Can I go now?

                    JIMMY

Sure.

                    ROSE

I'm kidding.

                    JIMMY

Asshole.

                    ROSE

You seem good. Are you good?

                    JIMMY

I'm great. You?

                    ROSE

I'm good… You know that speech you just gave would make most people weep and look for a loaded gun, but somehow it was almost attractive?

                    JIMMY

You wanna sleep around a little bit?

                    ROSE

Not even close.

Rose touches him.

                    ROSE

You know, maybe we're not so different.

                    JIMMY

Is that a good thing or a bad thing?

ROSE

I don't know.

Jimmy looks out toward the front door.

ROSE

You wanna go outside, give Zoey a few pushes, and say bye?

JIMMY

Like a normal family on the lawn with a swing? Yes. Very much so.

ROSE

Don't move. I'll be right back.

JIMMY

Okay.

Rose heads for the bedroom door, up left, then stops, and turns back.

ROSE

Hey.

Jimmy turns back to her.

ROSE

You don't have to stay frozen in time.

She exits. Jimmy sits.

ROSE [OFFSTAGE]

Oh hey. I meant to tell you. I ran into your friend Tony Testone at the market the other day.

JIMMY

Oh yeah? How's he doing? I haven't heard from him in a while.

ROSE [OFFSTAGE]

He's really good. That's why I wanted to tell you. He's with this really nice young girl. They're engaged. She's pregnant.

JIMMY

Get out a here?

ROSE [OFFSTAGE]

No. It was really nice to see. Really interesting girl. Strange name though. You ever heard of someone being named Binki?

JIMMY

No.

Rose steps back out onto the stage holding up the vintage Harley shirt.

ROSE

Hope you don't mind. Been meaning to grab this.

Jimmy stands.

JIMMY

It's yours. Just been holing it for you.

ROSE

Thanks.

Jimmy picks up Zoey's bag and follows Rose as they head for the front door.

JIMMY

It's been washed.

ROSE

What?

JIMMY

Never mind.

They exit.

LIGHTS OUT

THE END